W9-CHL-135

Envision It! | Visual Skills Handbook

Author's Purpose

Cause and Effect

Compare and Contrast

Sequence

Author's Purpose

Inform

Entertain

Cause and Effect

Cause

Effect

Compare and Contrast

Sequence

Envision It! | Visual Strategies Handbook

Background Knowledge

Important Ideas

Inferring

Monitor and Clarify

Predict and Set Purpose

Questioning

Story Structure

Summarize

Text Structure

Visualize

Background Knowledge

Let's Think About Reading!

- What do I already know?
- What does this remind me of?

Important Ideas

Let's Think About Reading!

- What is important to know?

Inferring

Let's Think About Reading!

- What do I already know?
- How does this help me understand what happened?

Monitor and Clarify

Let's Think About Reading!

- What does not make sense?
- How can I fix it?

Predict and Set Purpose

Let's Think About Reading!

- What do I already know?
- What do I think will happen?
- What is my purpose for reading?

Questioning

Let's Think About Reading!

- What questions do I have about what I am reading?

Story Structure

Let's Think About Reading!

- What happens in the beginning?
- What happens in the middle?
- What happens in the end?

Summarize

Let's Think About Reading!

- What happens in the story?
- What is the story mainly about?

Text Structure

Let's Think About Reading!

- How is the story organized?
- Are there any patterns?

Visualize

Let's Think About Reading!

- What pictures do I see in my mind?

Program Authors

Peter Afflerbach
Camille Blachowicz
Candy Dawson Boyd
Elena Izquierdo
Connie Juel
Edward Kame'enui
Donald Leu
Jeanne R. Paratore
P. David Pearson
Sam Sebesta
Deborah Simmons
Alfred Tatum
Sharon Vaughn
Susan Watts Taffe
Karen Kring Wixson

PEARSON
Glenview, Illinois • Boston, Massachusetts • Chandler, Arizona •
Upper Saddle River, New Jersey

We dedicate Reading Street to
Peter Jovanovich.

His wisdom, courage,
and passion for education
are an inspiration to us all.

About the Cover Artist
Daniel Moreton lives in New York City, where he uses his computer to create illustrations for books. When he is not working, Daniel enjoys cooking, watching movies, and traveling. On a trip to Mexico, Daniel was inspired by all of the bright colors around him. He likes to use those colors in his art.

Acknowledgments appear on page 218, which constitute an extension of this copyright page.
Copyright © 2011 by Pearson Education, Inc., or its affiliates. All Rights Reserved. Printed in the United States of America. This publication is protected by copyright, and permission should be obtained from the publisher prior to any prohibited reproduction, storage in a retrieval system, or transmission in any form or by any means, electronic, mechanical, photocopying, recording, or likewise. For information regarding permissions, write to Pearson Curriculum Group Rights & Permissions, One Lake Street, Upper Saddle River, New Jersey 07458.

Pearson, Scott Foresman, and Pearson Scott Foresman are trademarks, in the U.S. and/or other countries, of Pearson Education, Inc., or its affiliates.

ISBN-13: 978-0-328-45556-0
ISBN-10: 0-328-45556-3
4 5 6 7 8 9 10 V042 14 13 12 11
CC1

Dear Reader,

Are you enjoying your travels along *Scott Foresman Reading Street?* What new skills have you learned to help you read and understand new things? What strategies have helped you smooth out the "bumps in the road" as you read?

As you continue along *Reading Street,* you will read about people in communities at home, in school, and in neighborhoods. You will also read about communities in nature.
So buckle your seat belt
and enjoy the trip!

Sincerely,
The Authors

Unit 2 Contents

Communities

THE BIG Q

What is a community?

Week 1

Let's Talk About People in Communities 12

Let's Listen for Sounds 14

Phonics and High-Frequency Words 16

animal fantasy • social studies

Max and Ruby: A Big Fish for Max 20

written and designed by Rosemary Wells

illustrated by Jody Wheeler

Let's Write It! 36

literary nonfiction • social studies

At Home 38

Let's Learn It! 42

Week 2

Let's Talk About People in Communities 44

Let's Listen for Sounds 46

Phonics and High-Frequency Words 48

realistic fiction • social studies

The Farmer in the Hat 52

by Pat Cummings

Let's Write It! 68

expository text • social studies

Helping Hands at 4-H 70

by Lindy Russell

Let's Learn It! 76

Week 3

Let's Talk About People in Communities 78

Let's Listen for Sounds 80

Phonics and High-Frequency Words 82

expository text • social studies

Who Works Here? 86

by Melissa Blackwell Burke illustrated by Tim Spransy

Let's Write It! 98

procedural text • social studies

Neighborhood Map 100

Let's Learn It! 102

Unit 2 Contents

Week 4

Let's Talk About Communities in Nature 104

Let's Listen for Sounds 106

Phonics and High-Frequency Words 108

fiction • science

The Big Circle 112

by Eric Kimmel illustrated by Richard Bernal

Let's Write It! 130

literary nonfiction • science

We Are Safe Together 132

by Julia Nasser illustrated by Chris Boyd

Let's Learn It! 136

Week 5

Let's Talk About Communities in Nature 138

Let's Listen for Sounds 140

Phonics and High-Frequency Words 142

expository text • science

Life in the Forest 146

by Claire Daniel

Let's Write It! 162

magazine article • science

A Mangrove Forest 164

by Terry Lynk illustrated by Russell Farrell

Let's Learn It! 168

Week 6

Let's Talk About Communities in Nature 170

Let's Listen for Sounds 172

Phonics and High-Frequency Words 174

expository text • science

Honey Bees 178

by Jesús Cervantes illustrated by Tom Leonard

Let's Write It! 196

poetry

Poetry Collection 198

Under a Rock by Betsy Franco

Night Song by Leland B. Jacobs

Let's Learn It! 200

Pictionary 202

Tested Words 214

The Alphabet 216

High-Frequency Words 219

Envision It! A Comprehension Handbook

Envision It! Visual Skills Handbook EI•1–EI•6

Envision It! Visual Strategies Handbook EI•7–EI•18

READING STREET The Digital Path!

Don Leu
The Internet Guy

Right before our eyes, the nature of reading and learning is changing. The Internet and other technologies create new opportunities, new solutions, and new literacies. New reading comprehension skills are required online. They are increasingly important to our students and our society.

Those of us on the Reading Street team are here to help you on this new, and very exciting, journey.

See It!

- Big Question Video
- Concept Talk Video

- Envision It! Animations
- eReaders

- Interactive Sound-Spelling Cards

Hear It!

- *Sing with Me* Animations
- eSelections
- Grammar Jammer

- Vocabulary Activities

Get Online!
www.ReadingStreet.com

Concept Talk Video

Do It!

- Journal Word Bank
- Story Sort
- Letter Tile Drag and Drop
- Online Assessment
- Vocabulary Activities

Unit 2

Communities

Reading Street Online

www.ReadingStreet.com

- Big Question Video
- eSelections
- Envision It! Animations
- Story Sort

THE BIG ?

What is a community?

connect to SOCIAL STUDIES

A Big Fish for Max ANIMAL FANTASY

What does a family do together?

Paired Selection

At Home LITERARY NONFICTION

connect to SOCIAL STUDIES

The Farmer in the Hat REALISTIC FICTION

How is a school a community?

Paired Selection

Helping Hands at 4-H EXPOSITORY TEXT

connect to SOCIAL STUDIES

Who Works Here? EXPOSITORY TEXT

Who works to make our community a nice place?

Paired Selection

Neighborhood Map PROCEDURAL TEXT

connect to SCIENCE

The Big Circle FICTION

How do animal communities work together to survive?

Paired Selection

We Are Safe Together LITERARY NONFICTION

connect to SCIENCE

Life in the Forest EXPOSITORY TEXT

How are plant and animal communities important to each other?

Paired Selection

A Mangrove Forest MAGAZINE ARTICLE

connect to SCIENCE

Honey Bees EXPOSITORY TEXT

How is an insect community like a community of people?

Paired Selection

"Under a Rock" and "Night Song" POETRY

Objectives

- Listen closely to speakers and ask questions to help you better understand the topic.
- Share information and ideas about the topic. Speak at the correct pace.

Oral Vocabulary

Let's Talk About

People in Communities

- Share ideas about families as communities.
- Take part in a discussion about what a family does together.

READING STREET ONLINE CONCEPT TALK VIDEO
www.ReadingStreet.com

You've learned
094
Amazing Words
so far this year!

Objectives

• Pick out sounds at the beginning, in the middle, and at the end of one-syllable words. • Break up one-syllable words into each sound that makes up the word.

Phonemic Awareness

Let's Listen for Sounds

Read Together

- Find three things that begin with the sound /sh/. Say each sound in the words.
- Find something that ends with the sound /sh/. Say the ending sound.
- Find two things that begin with the sound /th/. Say the beginning sound.
- Find three things that rhyme with *tall*. Say the sound in the middle of those words.

READING STREET ONLINE SOUND-SPELLING CARDS
www.ReadingStreet.com

Objectives

- Decode words that use two or more consonants together to stand for one sound.
- Identify and read at least 100 words from a list of words that you use often.

Envision It! Sounds to Know

shark

sh

thermometer

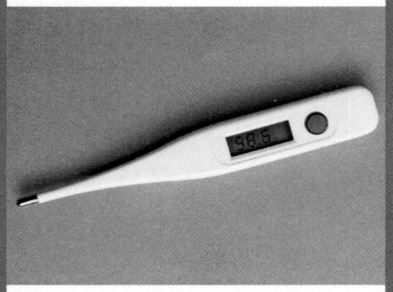

th

feather

th

READING STREET ONLINE SOUND-SPELLING CARDS
www.ReadingStreet.com

Phonics

Consonant Digraphs *sh, th*

Words I Can Blend

th	i	s
p	a	th
f	i	sh
w	i	th
sh	o	p

Sentences I Can Read

1. This path ends at Black Hill.
2. Can Pen sell fish with us at the shop?

Words I Can Read

said

want

good

catch

no

put

Sentences I Can Read

1. That man said he did want to catch a good nap.

2. No, Beth can not put that bell on this shelf.

Objectives

• Decode words by using common spelling patterns. • Identify and read at least 100 words from a list of words that you use often.

Envision It! | Sounds to Know

ball

a

chalk

al

READING STREET ONLINE SOUND-SPELLING CARDS
www.ReadingStreet.com

Phonics

Vowel Sound in *ball: a, al*

Words I Can Blend

a l l

w a l k

h a l l

t a l l

t a l k

Sentences I Can Read

1. All kids must walk in the hall.
2. That tall man can talk with Jan.

I Can Read!

Last fall, my math class had a trip to Glen Hill Mall.

Mom said it was good that I went with them. She put cash in my hand and said, "I want a small gift for Max. Can you get it?"

No one can catch a ball like Max. I got a swell mitt for him at this fun shop.

You've learned

- Consonant Digraphs *sh, th*
- Vowel Sound in *ball: a, al*

High-Frequency Words

said want good
catch no put

Genre

An **animal fantasy** is a story with animals that act like people. Next you will read about Max and Ruby—rabbits that go fishing.

Read Together

Max and Ruby

A Big Fish for Max

written and designed by
Rosemary Wells

illustrated
by Jody Wheeler

Question of the Week

What does a family do together?

"I wish I had a fish to eat," said Max.

"Then we will catch a big fish,"
said Grandma.

"We can walk to the park," said Ruby.

"And Max will catch a big fish."

"Good," said Max. "Yum, yum, yum!"

The path in the park led to the pond.

"Max can fish in this pond," said Ruby.

Max sat.
He got a red ball in his net.
But no fish bit.

Then Max got a black ship in his net.
But no fish bit.

And then Max got a clam shell
in his net.

"I want to call the fish," said Ruby.
"Then I can talk to the fish."
But still no fish bit.

"Well, we can all walk to the fish shop," said Grandma.
"And we can talk to the fish man."

The fish man had lots of fish in a box.
"We want a fresh fish," said Grandma.
"That fat fish is good."

At home, Grandma put the fish
in a hot pan.
Then Ruby put the fish in a dish.

"Yum, yum, yum!" said Max.

Objectives

- Describe the problem and the solution of a story. Retell a story's beginning, middle, and end in the order in which the events happened. • Read on your own for a period of time. • Connect what you read to your own experiences, other texts, and the world around you.

Envision It! Retell

READING STREET ONLINE
STORY SORT
www.ReadingStreet.com

Think Critically

1. Max, Ruby, and Grandma care about each other. How do you show you care for others? Text to Self

2. Was this story funny or serious? Why do you think so? Author's Purpose

3. What is the first thing that Max gets in his net? Sequence

4. Did you predict how Max would get a big fish? Was your prediction correct?

Predict and Set Purpose

5. Look Back and Write

Look back at pages 30 and 31. Where does Max get a big fish? Write about it. Use evidence from the story to support your answer.

TEST PRACTICE Extended Response

Meet the Author

Rosemary Wells

Ms. Wells says, "Some of my most pleasurable memories as a child were of fishing with my father. We used to catch snapper blues, and my mother cooked them in parsley and butter that night. Today fish is still one of my favorite things to eat."

When Rosemary Wells writes stories about Max and Ruby, she thinks about what her own two girls said and did when they were children.

Here are other books by Rosemary Wells.

Use the Reading Log in the *Reader's and Writer's Notebook* to record your independent reading.

Objectives

- Write short letters that put your ideas in an order that makes sense and uses the correct features.
- Understand and use nouns when reading, writing, and speaking.

Read Together

Let's Write It!

Key Features of a Friendly Letter

- begins with a greeting and ends with a closing
- often tells how the writer feels

READING STREET ONLINE
GRAMMAR JAMMER
www.ReadingStreet.com

Friendly Letter

You write a **friendly letter** to someone you know well. You can tell the person things about you. The student model on the next page is an example of a friendly letter.

Writing Prompt Think about things your family does together. Write a letter to persuade someone in your family to do something with you.

Writer's Checklist

Remember, you should . . .

- ✓ start your letter with a friendly greeting.
- ✓ give the reader reasons to do something with you.
- ✓ put your sentences in an order that makes sense.

Student Model

Dear Mom,
I like to walk to the park.
Can you please walk with me?
We can see trees and birds.
We can ride a boat in the pond.
It will be fun.
Your son,
Marco

Genre Friendly Letter
The letter begins with **Dear Mom.**

This **noun, boat,** names a thing.

Writing Trait Organization
The sentences are in an order that makes sense.

Conventions

Nouns

Remember A **noun** names a person, a place, an animal, or a thing.

The word **man** names a person. **Home** names a place. **Fox** names an animal. **Net** names a thing.

Objectives

- Figure out whether a story is true or make-believe and explain why.

Social Studies in Reading

Read Together

Genre

Literary Nonfiction

- Literary nonfiction is narrative text that tells about real people, places, and events. It is told like a story.
- Literary nonfiction can be a biography, or a story about someone's life.
- Literary nonfiction can be an autobiography, or a story about someone's life written by that person.
- As you read "At Home," think about what you know about literary nonfiction.

At Home

Plants use water.
Plants use the sun.
I want to help plants.

Dad puts pots on the shelf.

Let's Think About...

Who do you think is telling us about plants and pots? **Literary Nonfiction**

Mom cuts the grass.

Let's Think About...

Do you think this selection is true or a fantasy? Explain why. **Literary Nonfiction**

Sis can catch Gus.
We talk and have fun.

Objectives
- Read fluent
at your gr
and use
calle
w

Let's Think About...

What makes this selection literary nonfiction?
Literary Nonfiction

Let's Think About...

Reading Across Texts How are the families in *A Big Fish for Max* and "At Home" alike?

Writing Across Texts Write sentences about what the family in *A Big Fish for Max* likes to do and what the family in "At Home" likes to do.

y and understand texts de level. • Understand words that name actions, d *verbs*. Understand and use ords that name people, places, or things, called *nouns*. • Identify and put words into groups based on what they mean. • Understand and use nouns when reading, writing, and speaking. • Understand and use time-order words when reading, writing, and speaking. • Listen closely to speakers and ask questions to help you better understand the topic.

Read Together

Let's Learn It!

READING STREET ONLINE VOCABULARY ACTIVITIES
www.ReadingStreet.com

One of the best days of my life was when I won the big race. First, I stood at the starting line. Next, our coach said, "Go!" I ran as fast as I could. I was the winner!

Get Ready For Grade 2

Use words such as *first, next,* and *last* when speaking.

Listening and Speaking

Relate an Experience in Sequence When we tell about things that happen to us, we use words such as *first, next,* and *last*. When we listen to others, we ask questions if we don't understand.

Practice It! Think of something exciting that happened to you. Tell others what happened first, next, and last. Use nouns to name things.

Vocabulary

A singular **noun** names a person, animal, place, or thing. We can identify and sort nouns into word groups that name people, animals, places, or things.

Practice It! Read these singular nouns. Identify and sort them into the categories of people, animals, places, or things.

fish **ball** **shop** **boy**

Fluency

Accuracy and Rate Read the sentences. Say the word you see. Blend the sounds to read the word. Put the word in the sentence. Ask yourself if it makes sense.

Practice It!

1. That was a good walk.

2. All the fish in the pond want to swim.

3. Jan put small shells in her bag.

Objectives

- Listen closely to speakers and ask questions to help you better understand the topic.
- Share information and ideas about the topic. Speak at the correct pace.

Oral Vocabulary

Read Together

Let's Talk About

People in Communities

- Share ideas about schools as communities.
- Share ideas about a classroom community.

READING STREET ONLINE
CONCEPT TALK VIDEO
www.ReadingStreet.com

You've learned
102
Amazing Words
so far this year!

Objectives

- Say a group of words that rhyme using different groups of letters.
- Tell the difference between long- and short-vowel sounds in words that have one syllable.
- Combine sounds together to say words with one and two syllables.

Phonemic Awareness

Let's Listen for

Read Together

Sounds

- Find three things that rhyme with *take*.
- Find something that rhymes with *tap*. Now change the short *a* sound to a long *a* sound. Say the new word.
- Find two things that rhyme with *space*. Say the sounds in each word.
- Find two things that begin with the sound /j/.

READING STREET ONLINE
SOUND-SPELLING CARDS
www.ReadingStreet.com

Objectives

- Decode words by using letter-sound patterns to understand the different sounds vowels make.
- Decode words that end in with a silent "e".
- Identify and read at least 100 words from a list of words that you use often.

Envision It! Sounds to Know

rake

a_e

READING STREET ONLINE SOUND-SPELLING CARDS
www.ReadingStreet.com

Phonics

Long *a*: *a_e*

Words I Can Blend

b r a v e

m a d e

t r a d e

w a k e

b a k e

Sentences I Can Read

1. That brave man made him trade.
2. Will Nat wake up and bake it?

Words I Can Read

could

be

old

paper

of

horse

Sentences I Can Read

1. Could it be that this old box is made of paper?

2. Take this black horse and place it in the shade, Jake.

Objectives

- Decode words with consonants.
- Decode words that end in with a silent "e".

Envision It! Sounds to Know

cereal

c

giraffe

g

READING STREET ONLINE SOUND-SPELLING CARDS
www.ReadingStreet.com

Phonics

Consonants *c/s/, g/j/*

Words I Can Blend

r	a	c	e	
p	a	c	e	
p	a	g	e	
g	e	m		
c	e	n	t	s

Sentences I Can Read

1. Kate ran that race at a fast pace.
2. Did Dave spot that gem on page one that costs ten cents?

I Can Read!

Gabe saves old stuff. He kept an old pad of paper. Its last page had space for him to trace a face on it.

Gabe asks, "Could this page be a horse mask?"

Mom said, "Get rid of it!"

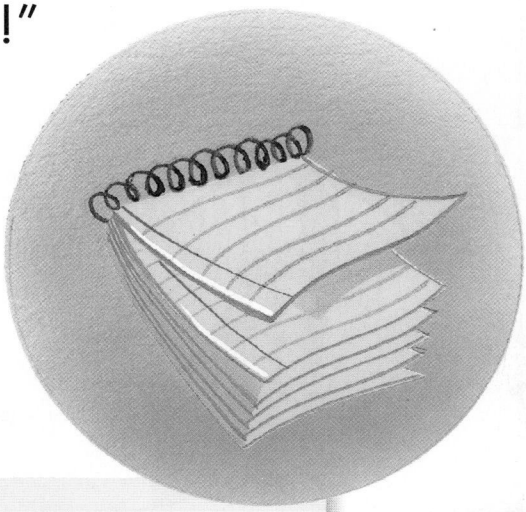

You've learned

- Long *a*: *a_e*
- Consonants *c*/s/, *g*/j/

High-Frequency Words

could be old
paper of horse

The Farmer in the Hat

by Pat Cummings

Read Together

Genre **Realistic fiction** has characters that act like real people. You will read a story about classmates putting on a play.

Question of the Week

How is a school a community?

Beth got the hat. "I could be the farmer, Old MacDonald, in this play," said Beth.

"But I am the farmer, Beth," said Dave.

"You can be a pig," said Beth.
"A pig!" Dave made an odd face.

Grace went up on stage.
"Let us make paper masks of faces," she said. "Ducks, hens, a pig, a horse!"

"I have the hat!" said Max.
"Beth is not the farmer!"

"I will take that hat, Max!"
Dave said.

"Stop it, Max and Dave!" said
Grace. "Let us make masks."

On his page, Max made a duck mask with tape. Beth made hens.

Dave made a pig mask on his page.

"That is an odd pig," Grace said.

"It takes ages to make this horse mask, Meg," said Jake.

"I can make this mask fast, Jake," said Meg.

Meg made a fat gerbil mask.

"Place that gerbil in a paper cage."
Jake gave a grin.

"Take your places up on stage," said Grace.

"Grunt!" Dave had on his pig mask.

"Squeak!" said Meg.

"Quack!" Max had on his duck mask.

"Cluck!" Beth had on her hen mask.

"Look at that cat!" said Grace.
"That is an odd farmer!"

Objectives

- Describe the problem and the solution of a story. Retell a story's beginning, middle, and end in the order in which the events happened. • Read on your own for a period of time.

Envision It! Retell

READING STREET ONLINE
STORY SORT
www.ReadingStreet.com

Think Critically

1. If you were in Beth's class, which character in the play would you be? **Text to Self**

2. Why do you think the author waited until the end to show the cat? **Think Like an Author**

3. Why did the children forget about the farmer's hat?

Cause and Effect

4. Look back on page 63. What clues could you use from the picture or the words to find out what a gerbil is? **Monitor and Clarify**

5. Look Back and Write
Look back at pages 60–63. Write about an actor in the play. Use evidence in the selection to support your answer.

TEST PRACTICE **Extended Response**

Pat Cummings

Pat Cummings once played a rabbit in a school play, and her sister played a grasshopper. Ms. Cummings made the cat the farmer in this story because "cats seem to naturally find the center of attention."

Ms. Cummings loves writing children's books. "The best part is that I can explore almost any subject."

Here are other books by Pat Cummings.

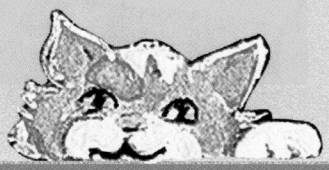

Use the Reading Log in the *Reader's and Writer's Notebook* to record your independent reading.

Objectives
• Write short nonfiction essays about topics you like. • Understand and use nouns when reading, writing, and speaking. • Use capitalization for names of people.

Read Together

Let's Write It!

Key Features of a Brief Composition

- tells interesting facts
- tells about one topic

READING STREET ONLINE
GRAMMAR JAMMER
www.ReadingStreet.com

Brief Composition

A **brief composition** tells information about real people or things. The student model on the next page is an example of a brief composition.

Writing Prompt Think about ways children work together at school. Now write about one thing children at your school do together.

Writer's Checklist

Remember, you should ...

- ✓ write about a real thing that children do together at your school.
- ✓ write in complete sentences.
- ✓ include at least one proper noun in your composition.

Student Model

Every Friday we clean our classroom at Parker School.

We make our desks neat. Eric wipes the board. Jo puts books away.

We keep our room clean. We like to help.

Writing Trait Sentences

This composition is made up of complete **sentences.**

The name *Eric* is an example of a **proper noun**.

Genre Composition

This **brief composition** tells about real people.

Conventions

Proper Nouns

Remember Special names for people, places, animals, and things are called **proper nouns**. Proper nouns begin with capital letters.

Max took the hat from **B**eth.

Objectives

• Tell the main idea of an article that you heard or read. • Figure out the important facts or details in an article or story that you heard or read.

Social Studies in Reading

Read Together

Genre

Expository Text

- Expository text is informational text that tells about real people, animals, places, or events.
- An expository text selection has a main idea. The main idea is the most important idea in the selection. Facts or details tell more about the main idea.
- An expository text selection usually has photographs that help explain the words.
- As you read "Helping Hands at 4-H," think about what you know about expository text. Then tell the main idea.

Helping Hands at 4-H

by Lindy Russell

Where could you see what farmers do? At a 4-H club!

How old are kids in 4-H? They can be ages 8 to 18.

At 4-H you can take care of a horse or a pig.

Let's Think About...

What facts or details do you learn on these two pages?
Expository Text

Let's Think About...

How does the photograph help you understand the words on this page?
Expository Text

You can get the eggs from the hens.

This 4-H club has a bake sale. They place an ad in the paper. They sell eggs too.

Let's Think About...

What details does the photograph tell that the words do not? **Expository Text**

The sale is good!
The club will get chicks.

Let's Think About...

What is the main idea of this selection?
Expository Text

The chicks will get big. Then the club will have lots of eggs to sell.

Let's Think About...

What facts or details tell more about the main idea?
Expository Text

Let's Think About...

Reading Across Texts In *The Farmer in the Hat* and "Helping Hands at 4-H," groups of children work together. What is each group trying to do? Why?

Writing Across Texts The children in both groups work well together. Why is that important? Write your ideas.

Objectives

• Read fluently and understand texts at your grade level. • Understand and use nouns when reading, writing, and speaking. • Understand and use time-order words when reading, writing, and speaking. • Share information and ideas about the topic. Speak at the correct pace.

Read Together

Let's Learn It!

READING STREET ONLINE VOCABULARY ACTIVITIES
www.ReadingStreet.com

Classroom Rules
- We take turns.
- We raise our hand before we speak.
- We keep our desks clean.

Get Ready For Grade 2

Answer a listener's questions.

Listening and Speaking

Share Information and Ideas When we share information and ideas, we speak clearly. We tell others important details. We answer questions if listeners do not understand.

Practice It! Think of two classroom rules. Tell the rules to others. Speak clearly and slowly, using people's names and the conventions of language.

Vocabulary

When we want to describe when things happen, we use **time-order words.**

Practice It! Read these words. Write sentences using each word.

yesterday **today** **tomorrow**

Fluency

Appropriate Phrasing When you see an exclamation mark at the end of a sentence, use your voice to show a strong feeling.

Practice It!

1. Look! Pat made a paper mask!

2. I did not think the skit could be this fun!

3. Run! We could be late for the play!

Objectives

- Listen closely to speakers and ask questions to help you better understand the topic.
- Share information and ideas about the topic. Speak at the correct pace.

Oral Vocabulary

Let's Talk About

Read Together

People in Communities

- Share ideas about people in our community.
- Discuss who works to make our community a nice place.
- Share information about jobs people have in our community.

READING STREET ONLINE
CONCEPT TALK VIDEO
www.ReadingStreet.com

You've learned

110

Amazing Words

so far this year!

Objectives

• Tell the difference between long- and short-vowel sounds in words that have one syllable. • Combine sounds together to say words with one and two syllables. • Pick out sounds at the beginning, in the middle, and at the end of one-syllable words.

Phonemic Awareness

Let's Listen for

Read Together

Sounds

- Find three things that begin with the sound /ch/. Say each sound in the words.
- Find something that rhymes with *sit*. Now change the short *i* sound to a long *i* sound. Say the new word.
- Find something that begins with the same sound you hear at the beginning of the word *whip*.
- Find something that rhymes with *stone*. Say each sound in the word.
- Find two things that rhyme with *side*.

READING STREET ONLINE
SOUND-SPELLING CARDS
www.ReadingStreet.com

Harvest Festival

Objectives

- Decode words by using letter-sound patterns to understand the different sounds vowels make.
- Decode words that end in with a silent "e".
- Identify and read at least 100 words from a list of words that you use often.

Envision It! Sounds to Know

lime

i_e

READING STREET ONLINE SOUND-SPELLING CARDS
www.ReadingStreet.com

Phonics

Long *i*: *i_e*

Words I Can Blend

h	i	d	e	
p	i	l	e	
s	l	i	m	e
p	r	i	d	e
k	i	t	e	

Sentences I Can Read

1. That big bug came to hide in this pile of black slime.
2. Kip takes pride in his kite.

Words I Can Read

people

live

work

who

out

Sentences I Can Read

1. People who live in this place ride bikes to work.
2. Five mice ran out to hide on that vine.

Objectives

- Decode words that use two or more consonants together to stand for one sound.
- Identify and read at least 100 words from a list of words that you use often.

Envision It! | Sounds to Know

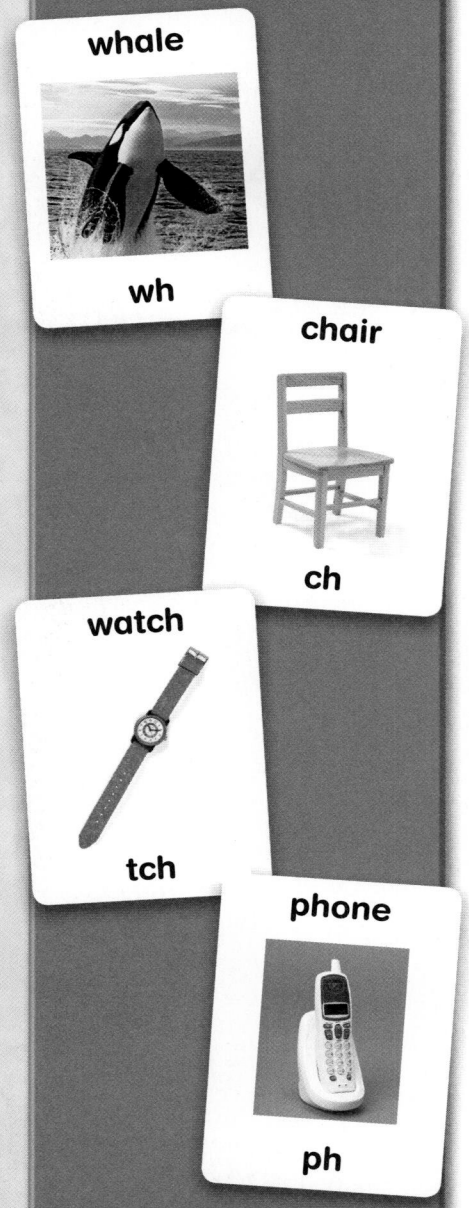

READING STREET ONLINE SOUND-SPELLING CARDS
www.ReadingStreet.com

Phonics

Digraphs *wh, ch, tch, ph*

Words I Can Blend

ch e ck

wh i ch

g r a ph

wh i t e

d i tch

Sentences I Can Read

1. Check which graph can help.
2. Did that white hat drop in the ditch?

I Can Read!

People who live on this lane like to work out. Mike and Chuck ride bikes. Phil and Jane run on the path.

Mom and Dad catch fish in Duck Lake. Beth swims. Jill hikes on the hill. Which is best?

You've learned

- Long *i*: *i_e*
- Consonant Digraphs *wh, ch, tch, ph*

High-Frequency Words

people live work
who out

Who Works Here?

by Melissa Blackwell Burke
illustrated by Tim Spransy

Genre

Expository text tells about real people and events. Next you will read about real people who live and work in a neighborhood. What do you want to find out? Set a purpose for reading.

Read Together

Question of the Week

Who works to make our community a nice place?

People live and work
in this neighborhood.
It is such a busy place.

Who works in this place?
Phil will talk to them.
They all like to help us.

I help us all stay safe.
When you ride your bike, stop
and check all ways.
I will help you cross.

I help stop fires. Fire can be bad.
All of us must be safe from fire.

I drop mail in this box. This man will stop and wave and smile. This man likes to chat a while.

I drive this big bus.
People can ride this big bus. This bus will stop and pick them up.

I pick up trash.
When it is set out,
I will pitch it in this big truck.

Who works where you live?
Smile at them like Phil.
You will like them!

Objectives

• Tell the main idea of an article that you heard or read. • Read on your own for a period of time. • Write short comments on stories, poems, and nonfiction articles that have information. • Connect what you read to your own experiences, other texts, and the world around you.

Envision It! | **Retell**

READING STREET ONLINE
STORY SORT
www.ReadingStreet.com

Think Critically

1. This selection is about workers in a community. What other community job might someone have?

Text to World

2. Why do you think the author used photographs in this selection? Think Like an Author

3. What do you think the author wants you to know?

Author's Purpose

4. What did you learn about workers in a community by reading this selection?

Important Ideas

5. Look Back and Write Look back at pages 90 and 91. Write about the job of one of the people you see.

TEST PRACTICE | Extended Response

Meet the Author

Read Together

Melissa Blackwell Burke

Melissa Blackwell Burke grew up in a small town in Texas. She loved to visit the library. She says, "When I was a little girl, I wanted to be many things, including a teacher, a newspaper reporter, and a librarian. I have been two of those—a teacher and a newspaper reporter. Who knows—I might still become a librarian some day!"

Here are other books about neighborhood workers.

Reading Log

Use the Reading Log in the *Reader's and Writer's Notebook* to record your independent reading.

Objectives

• Write short nonfiction essays about topics you like. • Understand and use nouns when reading, writing, and speaking. • Use capitalization for names of people.

Expository

Let's Write It!

Read Together

Key Features of an Explanation

- tells about a person, idea, or thing
- helps people understand the topic

READING STREET ONLINE
GRAMMAR JAMMER
www.ReadingStreet.com

Explanation

An **explanation** tells about real people, ideas, or things. It helps a reader understand the topic. The student model on the next page is an example of an explanation.

Writing Prompt Think about the jobs people do. Now think about a job you think is interesting. Write a brief explanation of the job.

Writer's Checklist

Remember, you should ...

- ✓ tell about what a real person does at work.
- ✓ use capital letters and punctuation correctly.
- ✓ capitalize titles, such as Mr., Mrs., Ms., or Dr.

Student Model

A Teacher's Job

Mrs. Taylor is a teacher.
She teaches children to read.
She teaches them how to do
math and spelling.
Mrs. Taylor loves children.

Writing Trait Conventions

Use capital letters for names when you write. Use periods at the end of sentences.

The **special title** *Mrs.* begins with a capital letter and ends with a period.

Genre Explanation

The author thinks a teacher's job is interesting. The author explains what a teacher does.

Conventions

Special Titles

A **title** can come before the name of a person. A title begins with a capital letter. Some titles end with a period.

Officer Black **Ms.** Timms **Dr.** Pak

Objectives

- Explain what different signs and symbols mean.

Social Studies in Reading

Read Together

Genre

Procedural Text

- Maps use words along with map features, including signs and symbols.
- Signs and symbols on a map help you know where you are and which way you can go.
- A compass rose is a symbol that shows you the directions north, east, south, and west. These directions are usually abbreviated N, E, S, and W.
- As you read "Neighborhood Map," think about what you've learned about signs and symbols in procedural text.

Neighborhood Map

This shows people where to wait for a bus.

This tells drivers to stop.

This tells drivers to let other drivers go first.

This means drivers may only drive in one direction on the street.

This means that a train may cross.

This means pedestrians may cross.

Let's Think About...

What signs do you see?
Procedural Text

Let's Think About...

What do the signs and symbols tell you?
Procedural Text

Let's Think About...

Reading Across Texts On the map, trace the route Phil takes as he meets the neighborhood workers.

Writing Across Texts Use the map. Write directions that tell Phil's route.

Objectives

• Read fluently and understand texts at your grade level. • Understand and use nouns when reading, writing, and speaking. • Listen closely to speakers and ask questions to help you better understand the topic. • Understand and use words that name directions.

Read Together

Let's Learn It!

READING STREET ONLINE VOCABULARY ACTIVITIES
www.ReadingStreet.com

Don't forget about our trip to the science museum on Friday! We will leave at 9:00 in the morning. Ms. Chase will collect money for ...

Get Ready For Grade 2

Make eye contact with listeners.

Listening and Speaking

Make Announcements When we make an announcement, we remember to speak loudly enough to be heard. We make eye contact with listeners. We tell all of the information.

Practice It! Make an announcement to the class about a field trip. Tell when you are going, where you are going, and what time you will leave. Use proper nouns, such as names of teachers.

Vocabulary

Direction words tell us where things are and how to get from place to place.

***Above* and *below* are direction words.**

Practice It! Write instructions on how to get from your classroom to the library. Use direction words.

Fluency

Appropriate Phrasing When you come to a period, you know it is the end of a sentence. Stop when you reach the period to show when the sentence ends.

Practice It!

1. I live with Mom, Dad, and Jack.

2. My cat likes to go out and catch mice.

Objectives

- Listen closely to speakers and ask questions to help you better understand the topic.
- Share information and ideas about the topic. Speak at the correct pace.

Oral Vocabulary

Read Together

Let's Talk About

Communities in Nature

- Share information about communities in nature.
- Share information about animals and animal behavior.
- Contribute to a discussion about how animal communities work together to survive.

READING STREET ONLINE
CONCEPT TALK VIDEO
www.ReadingStreet.com

You've learned
118
Amazing Words
so far this year!

Objectives

- Tell the difference between long- and short-vowel sounds in words that have one syllable.
- Break up one-syllable words into each sound that makes up the word.

Phonemic Awareness

Let's Listen for Sounds

Read Together

- Find something that rhymes with *nod*. Change the short *o* sound to a long *o* sound. Say the new word.
- Find five things that contain the long *o* sound.
- Find two things that rhyme with *cone*. Say the sounds in each word.

READING STREET ONLINE SOUND-SPELLING CARDS
www.ReadingStreet.com

Objectives

- Decode words by using letter-sound patterns to understand the different sounds vowels make.
- Decode words that end in with a silent "e".
- Identify and read at least 100 words from a list of words that you use often.

Envision It! Sounds to Know

rope

o_e

READING STREET ONLINE SOUND-SPELLING CARDS
www.ReadingStreet.com

Phonics

Long *o*: *o_e*

Words I Can Blend

s	t	o	n	e
b	r	o	k	e
h	o	p	e	
m	o	l	e	
h	o	l	e	

Sentences I Can Read

1. That stone broke the glass.
2. I hope that mole can spot its hole.

Words I Can Read

there

down

inside

now

together

Sentences I Can Read

1. Take down that note and place it there inside his desk.

2. Now those kids can all walk together.

Objectives

- Identify and read contractions.
- Identify and read at least 100 words from a list of words that you use often.

Envision It! Sounds to Know

can + not = can't

contraction

she + will = she'll

contraction

I + am = I'm

contraction

READING STREET ONLINE SOUND-SPELLING CARDS
www.ReadingStreet.com

Phonics

Contractions

Words I Can Blend

c a n 't

i t 'l l

i s n 't

I 'm

d i d n 't

Sentences I Can Read

1. It is odd that Lin can't tell if it'll be nice out, isn't it?
2. I'm glad Pam didn't get lost.

I Can Read!

Josh and Grace spoke on the phone together. Josh is sick, and he'll rest inside for now.

Grace said, "That's too bad. There is class work that you'll want. Let's get together. I'm close and can get it down to you."

You've learned

- Long *o*: *o_e*
- Contractions

High-Frequency Words

there down inside
now together

The Big Circle

by Eric Kimmel
illustrated by Richard Bernal

Genre Stories that are **fiction** are made-up stories. Next you will read a made-up story about dinosaurs.

Question of the Week

How do animal communities work together to survive?

Big T. Rex wakes up.
Big T. Rex wants his lunch,
but not bones and not stones.

Big T. Rex wants meat.

This is a herd of triceratops.
This herd is walking home.

At home this herd can get grass. Munching grass at home will make them fat.

Sniff, sniff. Big T. Rex smells with his nose. "Hmm," said Big T. Rex.

"This nose smells a baby. I can hunt it. I'll get it and it will make a good lunch. Yum, yum!"

Big T. Rex rose up on his back legs.
Big T. Rex ran up the slope and down.
The herd saw Big T. Rex run.

It was time to make a big circle. The small animals went inside the circle. The baby went inside too.

Big T. Rex didn't like this.
Big T. Rex couldn't get his lunch.

But Big T. Rex didn't quit.
"I'll make them run."

But the herd didn't run.
They kept still and close together
in the big circle.

Then they gave Big T. Rex a poke and a bump. They drove him back.

Big T. Rex ran back up the slope. Those triceratops saw Big T. Rex run. Now all are safe.

They will walk home and then munch grass there. Big T. Rex can't get them. The herd is safe.

Objectives

- Describe the problem and the solution of a story. Retell a story's beginning, middle, and end in the order in which the events happened. • Read on your own for a period of time.
- Make inferences about what you read using details to support your ideas.

Envision It! | Retell

READING STREET ONLINE
STORY SORT
www.ReadingStreet.com

Think Critically

1. How do other kinds of animals protect their babies? **Text to World**

2. What does the author want you to learn in this story? **Author's Purpose**

3. What happened after Big T. Rex saw the baby triceratops? **Sequence**

4. Why did the herd of triceratops make a big circle? **Inferring**

5. Look Back and Write Look back at page 125. Write about how this animal community helped each other. Give evidence from the story to support your answer. Discuss what you wrote with a partner.

TEST PRACTICE | **Extended Response**

Eric Kimmel

As a boy, Eric Kimmel visited the Museum of Natural History in New York City almost every weekend. "The dinosaur skeletons were old friends," he says. "Triceratops and stegosaurus were my favorites."

Richard Bernal

Richard Bernal drew the pictures for this story. "I love dinosaurs," he says. "I have several dinosaur toys in my studio."

Here are other books by Eric Kimmel and Richard Bernal.

Use the Reading Log in the *Reader's and Writer's Notebook* to record your independent reading.

Objectives
• Write short poems that have details one can see, smell, hear, taste, or touch. • Understand and use nouns when reading, writing, and speaking.

Read Together

Let's Write It!

Key Features of a Poem

- it can describe an event
- the lines may rhyme

READING STREET ONLINE
GRAMMAR JAMMER
www.ReadingStreet.com

Poem

A **poem** is a short piece of writing. The writer uses lines of well-chosen words. Some words in poems may rhyme.

Writing Prompt Think about how animals protect themselves. Now write a poem about an animal that protects itself from an enemy.

Writer's Checklist

Remember, you should . . .

- ✓ tell how the animal protects itself.
- ✓ describe an event in an order that makes sense.
- ✓ make sure you begin proper nouns with a capital letter.
- ✓ say your poem aloud.

Student Model

It is Friday.
Fox wants lunch.
She needs to catch!
She likes to munch!
Hurry, Turtle! Time to hide!
Turtle must hide inside.
Turtle hides inside his shell.
Turtle can hide so well!

This **proper noun** begins with a capital letter.

Writing Trait Organization
The lines of the poem show what happens in sequence.

Genre
This **poem** has lines that rhyme to sound more interesting. Say the poem aloud.

Conventions

Days, Months, and Holidays

Remember Days of the week, **months**, and **holidays** all begin with capital letters.

Mother's Day is a **Sunday** in **May.**

Objectives

- Figure out whether a story is true or make-believe and explain why.

Science in Reading

Read Together

Genre

Literary Nonfiction

- Literary nonfiction tells about real people, animals, places, or events.
- Literary nonfiction has a main idea and facts or details that tell more about the main idea.
- Literary nonfiction usually has some elements of a story, such as characters, plot, or setting.
- Read "We Are Safe Together." What did you learn about literary nonfiction that helps you better understand this selection?

We Are Safe Together

by Julia Nasser
illustrated by Chris Boyd

a school of fish

I'm a fish. A lake is my home. I swim with many fish. I'm inside this big circle. We stick together to be safe.

I'm a baby zebra. Grassland is my home. There are big zebras in this herd. We can run fast. We stick together to be safe.

Let's Think About...

What clues on these pages tell you this is literary nonfiction?
Literary Nonfiction

I'm a bird. I bend down to dig up my lunch. I'm with my flock. We can go up fast. We stick together to be safe.

Let's Think About...

Is this selection true or a fantasy? How do you know?
Literary Nonfiction

a herd of triceratops

I'm a triceratops. I don't live here now. I ate grass and plants. I walked with a big herd. We stuck together to be safe.

Let's Think About...

What is the main idea of this selection? **Literary Nonfiction**

Let's Think About...

Reading Across Texts How is what happens in *The Big Circle* similar to what happens in "We Are Safe Together"?

Writing Across Texts Write the facts you learned about triceratops in *The Big Circle* and "We Are Safe Together."

Objectives

• Read fluently and understand texts at your grade level. • Identify and put words into groups based on what they mean. • Listen closely to speakers and ask questions to help you better understand the topic.

Let's Learn It!

Read Together

READING STREET ONLINE VOCABULARY ACTIVITIES
www.ReadingStreet.com

Listening and Speaking

Get Ready For Grade 2

Use good listening and speaking skills, even in conversations with friends.

Informal Conversations When we have conversations with friends, we pay attention to the speaker. We speak clearly when it is our turn to speak.

Practice It! Have a conversation with others about how animal communities work together to survive. Follow the rules. Speak clearly and slowly, using the conventions of language. Be a good listener and a good speaker.

Vocabulary

When we **sort words,** we put them into groups that make sense.

A *tiger* eats meat. A *zebra* eats plants.

Practice It! Read the names of these animals. Identify and sort them into groups of plant eaters and meat eaters.

lion **horse** **deer** **rabbit**

Fluency

Accuracy and Rate Read the sentences. When you read, read the words you see. Blend the sounds to read the word. Check by putting the new word in the sentence to see if it makes sense.

Practice It!

1. We'll write a note to Steph together.

2. I can't ride my bike down the hill.

3. Isn't it good to be inside the school?

Objectives

- Listen closely to speakers and ask questions to help you better understand the topic.
- Share information and ideas about the topic. Speak at the correct pace.

Oral Vocabulary

Read Together

Let's Talk About

Communities in Nature

- Share information about communities in nature.
- Share information about animals and plants.
- Share ideas about how plant and animal communities are important to each other.

READING STREET ONLINE
CONCEPT TALK VIDEO
www.ReadingStreet.com

You've learned
1 2 6
Amazing Words
so far this year!

Objectives

• Tell the difference between long- and short-vowel sounds in words that have one syllable. • Combine sounds together to say words with one and two syllables. • Break up one-syllable words into each sound that makes up the word.

Phonemic Awareness

Let's Listen for Sounds

Read Together

- Find four things that contain the long *u* sound. Say each sound in one of the words.
- Find something that rhymes with *rub*. Change the short *u* sound to a long *u* sound. Say the new word.
- Find something that contains the long *e* sound.

READING STREET ONLINE
SOUND-SPELLING CARDS
www.ReadingStreet.com

Objectives

- Decode words by using letter-sound patterns to understand the different sounds vowels make.
- Decode words that end in with a silent "e".
- Identify and read at least 100 words from a list of words that you use often.

Envision It! | Sounds to Know

mule

u_e

concrete

e_e

READING STREET ONLINE
SOUND-SPELLING CARDS
www.ReadingStreet.com

Phonics

Long *u*: *u_e*; Long *e*: *e_e*

Words I Can Blend

u s e

th e s e

P e t e

r u d e

r u l e

Sentences I Can Read

1. Jack can use these white socks.
2. Pete made a rule that kids can't act rude.

Words I Can Read

grow

food

around

find

water

under

Sentences I Can Read

1. Will food grow on this land around his home?

2. Steve can find cute fish under the water.

Objectives

• Read words that add endings to the main part of the word. • Identify and read at least 100 words from a list of words that you use often.

Envision It! Sounds to Know

filled

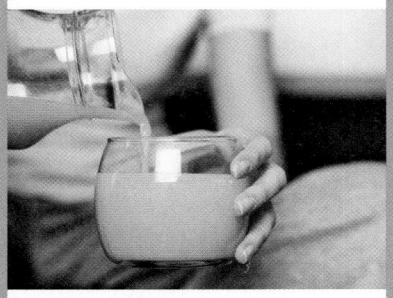

ending -ed

jumped

ending -ed

twisted

ending -ed

READING STREET ONLINE
SOUND-SPELLING CARDS
www.ReadingStreet.com

Phonics

Inflected Ending *-ed*

Words I Can Blend

c a l l e d

t a l k e d

m u n ch e d

a d d e d

p r i n t e d

Sentences I Can Read

1. Vic called Lill and talked as he munched on lunch.
2. Jon printed his name and added six and nine.

I Can Read!

Food can grow in odd places. June and Gene watched as fish munched on plants under water.

Pete helped us find snacks that bugs like around rocks. Dad planted yams in this big tub.

Plants can get big in many places. If these plants make food, let's find good places that they can grow.

You've learned

- Long *u*: *u_e;* Long *e*: *e_e*
- Inflected Ending *-ed*

High-Frequency Words

grow food around
find water under

Life in the Forest

by Claire Daniel

Read Together

Genre

Expository text tells facts about real places. Next you will read about the plants and animals in a forest.

Question of the Week

How are plant and animal communities important to each other?

We can find life in the forest.
It is a busy place!

Sun helped these leaves get wide and flat.

Sun shines on the leaves and helps them grow. Bugs like munching on them. Yum, yum! Bugs can eat lots and lots.

This woodpecker sits on a branch.
Peck! Peck! Peck!
It pecks to get at bugs.

These holes tell us that woodpeckers pecked on this tree.

This huge log is soft and damp.
Water has made this log rot.
Small bugs made homes in this log.

This bird hops on this log
and then pecks at it. Yum, yum!
It gets bugs when it pecks.

Nuts grow on trees and then fall all around. Squirrels get nuts and munch on them. Yum, yum!

A fox is cute, but it likes to catch small animals.

This black bear eats grass, nuts, and grubs. Grubs are small bugs that hide under rocks and logs.

This bear picked up these rocks and hunted for grubs.

This hummingbird uses its bill to get food. It sticks its bill in this plant.

Many plants have shapes like tubes. Small hummingbirds can sip from these plants.

Hummingbirds can catch small bugs too.

This big forest is filled with life.
Many animals and plants call it home.
It is a busy place!

Objectives

- Read on your own for a period of time.
- Say the main idea in your own words whether you heard it or read it.
- Make inferences about what you read using details to support your ideas.
- Connect what you read to your own experiences, other texts, and the world around you.

Envision It! Retell

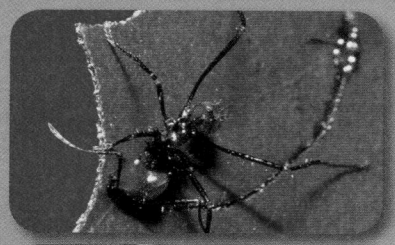

READING STREET ONLINE
STORY SORT
www.ReadingStreet.com

Think Critically

1. How are the dinosaurs in *The Big Circle* different from the animals mentioned in *Life in the Forest?* **Text to Text**

2. Why does the author use captions with some photographs? **Think Like an Author**

3. Why do you think the author wrote *Life in the Forest?* **Author's Purpose**

4. What did you already know about trees that helped you understand this selection? **Background Knowledge**

5. Look Back and Write Look back at pages 158 and 159. Write about one animal that lives in the forest. Use evidence from the selection to support your answer.

TEST PRACTICE **Extended Response**

Meet the Author

Read Together

Claire Daniel

Claire Daniel learned about forests on a three-month hiking trip with her husband. "That was an amazing experience—being in the forest and living in it."

A bear came to their campsite once. "We heard him coming, so we ran to a shelter. It was a frightening experience! The bear went into our tent and then backed out of it, not finding any food."

Here are more books by Claire Daniel.

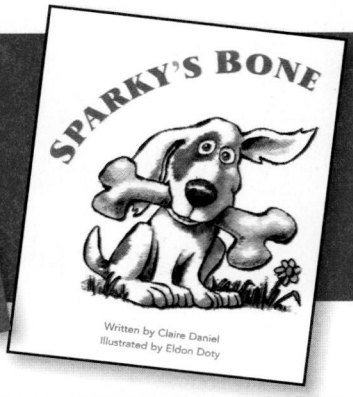

Reading Log

Use the Reading Log in the *Reader's and Writer's Notebook* to record your independent reading.

Objectives
• Write short nonfiction essays about topics you like. • Understand and use nouns when reading, writing, and speaking.

Read Together

Let's Write It!

Key Features of a Description

- tells about real people or things
- uses descriptive words
- can tell how things look

READING STREET ONLINE
GRAMMAR JAMMER
www.ReadingStreet.com

Description

A **description** tells about real things. It can tell how things look or sound. The student model on the next page is an example of a description.

Writing Prompt Think about how plants and animals are important to each other. Now write a description about how an animal uses plants to survive.

Writer's Checklist

Remember, you should . . .

- ✓ tell about a real animal and a real plant or plants.
- ✓ describe in words that tell how things look to you.
- ✓ add **-s** to make plural nouns that mean more than one.

Student Model

Squirrels Need Trees

Squirrels live in trees.

Squirrels eat the nuts that grow on trees.

I think squirrels look cute when they look for nuts.

These **nouns** that end in **-s** tell about more than one squirrel or tree or nut.

Writing Trait Voice
This writer shows voice by saying squirrels are cute.

Genre Description
This description tells about real squirrels.

Conventions

- **Singular and Plural Nouns**
- **Remember** Many nouns add **-s** to mean more than one. Say the plural nouns.
- **nut + s = nuts bug + s = bugs**

Objectives

- Say the main idea in your own words whether you heard it or read it.
- Identify and understand parts of a magazine article.

Science in Reading

Read Together

Genre

Magazine Article

- A magazine article is expository text that tells about a topic.
- The article has facts about the topic.
- The article may have pictures. They help us understand the topic.
- The article may also have a Table of Contents. The Table of Contents, including titles and page numbers, can help us locate specific information in the article.
- Read "A Mangrove Forest." As you read, look for elements of a magazine article.

A Mangrove Forest

by Terry Lynk
illustrated by Russell Farrell

Table of Contents

Animals . . . . . p. 164
Fish. . . . . p. 165
Food . . . . . p. 166
Save the Forests . . . . . p. 167

Animals

Lots of animals live here.
Some live in the water.
Some live out of the water.
They are all around this forest.

Fish

Have you watched fish swim under a tree?
You can find fish in this forest.
These trees grow in salt water.
Fish swim under the trees.

Let's Think About...

Find the Table of Contents. How can you use it to find information in this article?
Magazine Article

Let's Think About...

How can you use the title "Fish" in the Table of Contents to find information?
Magazine Article

Let's Think About...

What clues can you use from the picture or the words to find out who lives in the forest?
Magazine Article

Let's Think About...

What facts are on this page?
Magazine Article

Food

Fish find food in the water. Birds can use fish and bugs as food.

Save the Forests

Some forests like this are being lost. We must save these forests.

Let's Think About...

How does this photograph help you understand the article?
Magazine Article

Let's Think About...

What **important details** can you identify in the article?
Magazine Article

Let's Think About...

Reading Across Texts How are the forests in *Life in the Forest* and "A Mangrove Forest" alike? How are they different?

Writing Across Texts Write sentences about each forest.

Objectives

• Read fluently and understand texts at your grade level. • Understand and use words that name actions, called *verbs*. Understand and use words that name people, places, or things, called *nouns*. • Understand and use nouns when reading, writing, and speaking. • Share information and ideas about the topic. Speak at the correct pace.

Read Together

Let's Learn It!

READING STREET ONLINE
VOCABULARY ACTIVITIES
www.ReadingStreet.com

Get Ready For Grade 2

Use the conventions of language when sharing information.

Listening and Speaking

Share Information and Ideas When we share information and ideas with others, we speak clearly. When others share information and ideas with us, we listen carefully.

Practice It! Ask others how plant and animal communities help each other. Share your ideas. Speak clearly and slowly. Use plural nouns for things. Listen carefully.

Vocabulary

If a word has more than one meaning, you can use nearby words, or **context clues,** to understand which meaning is being used. The word *place* can mean "the space where someone or something is." *Place* can also mean "to put something somewhere."

Practice It! Read these sentences. What is the meaning of the word *place* in each sentence?

The forest is an amazing **place.**
The bird will **place** a twig on the nest.

Fluency

Appropriate Phrasing When you come to a period, you know it is the end of a sentence. Stop when you reach the period to show when the sentence ends.

Practice It!

1. Pete saw a bear eat his food.

2. The cute pup wanted to sip water.

• Listen closely to speakers and ask questions to help you better understand the topic. • Share information and ideas about the topic. Speak at the correct pace.

Oral Vocabulary

Let's Talk About

Communities in Nature

- Recall how people work together in a community.
- Share information about insects and insect behavior.
- Take part in a discussion about how an insect community is like a community of people.

READING STREET ONLINE
CONCEPT TALK VIDEO
www.ReadingStreet.com

You've learned
134
Amazing Words
so far this year!

Objectives

- Tell the difference between long- and short-vowel sounds in words that have one syllable.
- Combine sounds together to say words with one and two syllables.

Phonemic Awareness

Let's Listen for

Read Together

Sounds

- Find something that rhymes with *bed*. Change the short *e* sound to a long *e* sound. Say the new word.
- Find four things that contain the long *e* sound.
- Find three things that contain the short *a* sound and have two syllables.
- Find something that rhymes with *mitten*. Say each sound in the word.

READING STREET ONLINE
SOUND-SPELLING CARDS
www.ReadingStreet.com

Objectives

- Decode words by using letter-sound patterns to understand the different sounds vowels make.
- Decode words that use two vowels to make one sound.
- Identify and read at least 100 words from a list of words that you use often.

Envision It! | Sounds to Know

we

-e

bee

ee

READING STREET ONLINE
SOUND-SPELLING CARDS
www.ReadingStreet.com

Phonics

Long *e*: *e*, *ee*

Words I Can Blend

sh e

s ee

f ee l

w e

n ee d

Sentences I Can Read

1. Can't she see that we need that desk?
2. Pat ate too much and didn't feel well.

Words I Can Read

family

other

also

their

some

new

Sentences I Can Read

1. That bee family also can see the other side of that hive.

2. Their new home has some big trees.

Objectives

- Decode words that have syllables that end in consonants.
- Identify and read at least 100 words from a list of words that you use often.

Envision It! Sounds to Know

basket

VC/CV

READING STREET ONLINE SOUND-SPELLING CARDS
www.ReadingStreet.com

Phonics

Syllables VC/CV

Words I Can Blend

r a b b i t

b a s k e t

m i s t a k e

t a d p o l e

i n s i d e

Sentences I Can Read

1. We set his pet rabbit in its basket.
2. Will it be a mistake to keep that tadpole inside?

I Can Read!

Lee and Sam like to invent new stuff. When they see a need, these kids fix it. Their family admits some of the stuff is odd.

Lee made mittens for his pet reptile. He also invented zigzag buttons. Sam came up with a picnic basket for his kitten. Will Lee and Sam make other stuff? We will see!

You've learned

- Long *e: e, ee*
- Syllables VC/CV

High-Frequency Words

family other also
their some new

Honey Bees

by Jesús Cervantes
illustrated by Tom Leonard

Genre

Expository text tells facts about real people, places, animals, or things. This article tells about honey bees.

Question of the Week

How is an insect community like a community of people?

The sun shines. These honey bees wake up. It is time for these insects to work.

Buzz,
buzz,
buzz.

In the hive, bees live like a family. In the hive we can see there is a queen bee, lots of worker bees, and some drones.

This is the queen bee.
She rules the hive.

These bees are drones.
Drones help the queen bee.

This hive is hidden in a big tree.
Worker bees will keep this hive safe.

It is not wise to make bees mad! Mad bees will attack.

Worker bees make wax cells in the hive. These wax cells are small holes.

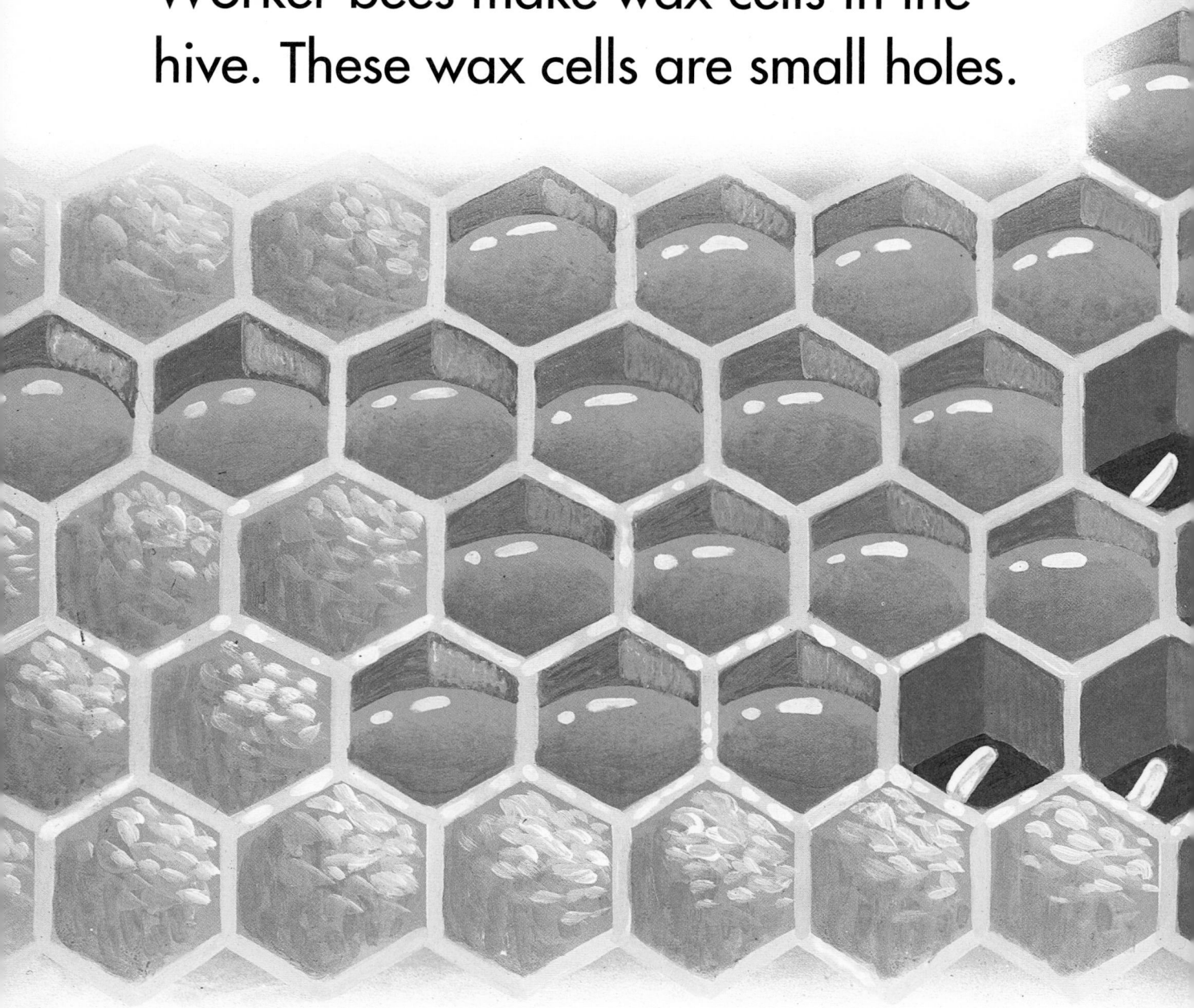

Bees save honey in some wax cells. Small bees live and grow big in other cells.

Bees feed on honey. Worker bees feed honey to other bees in the hive. Bees make honey from nectar.

Bees get nectar inside flowers.
Bees take this sweet nectar back home.

Bees also get pollen
from flowers.

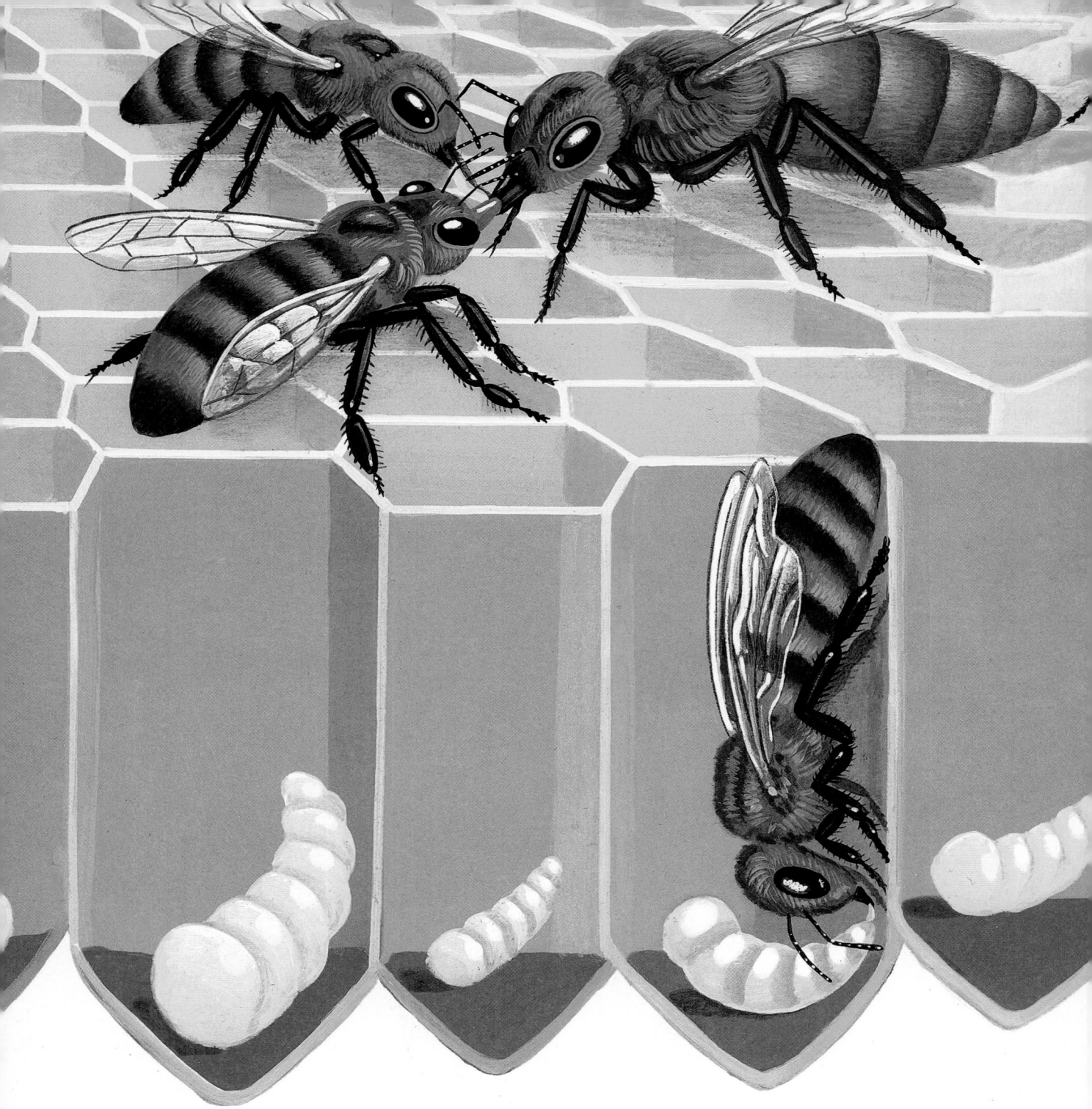

Worker bees feed pollen to
the queen bee and small bees.
It helps them get big.

When those small bees get big,
it is time to make a new hive.

Worker bees make the new hive.
A new queen bee will go with them.

When it gets cold, these bees will go inside their hive and sleep and rest. The bees will wake up when the sun shines.

Objectives
• Write short nonfiction essays about topics you like. • Understand and use nouns when reading, writing, and speaking.

Read Together

Let's Write It!

Key Features of an Expository Paragraph

- tells about and explains real things
- can describe the things

READING STREET ONLINE
GRAMMAR JAMMER
www.ReadingStreet.com

Expository Paragraph

An **expository paragraph** explains real things. The student model on the next page is an example of an expository paragraph.

Writing Prompt Think about another kind of insect that lives in a community. Now write a paragraph about that insect community.

Writer's Checklist

Remember, you should ...

- ✓ explain or describe a real insect community.
- ✓ write sentences about the topic.
- ✓ make sure each sentence in your paragraph has at least one noun.

Student Model

Ants

Ants live together. Little ants have big jobs. Some ants find food. Some ants take care of the queen.

This **noun**, **ants,** names a kind of insect. The sentence is about ants.

Writing Trait Focus
Each sentence is about the main topic.

Genre Expository Paragraph
This writer explains how ants live together.

Conventions

Nouns in Sentences

Remember **Nouns** name persons, places, animals, or things. A noun can be in more than one place in a sentence.

The **hives** are hidden in a **tree.**

Objectives

- Describe and use rhythm and rhyme in poetry.

Genre

Poetry

- A poem is written in lines. Lines of poetry form groups of lines. These groups of lines are called stanzas.
- A poem often rhymes. This means words at the ends of some lines have the same middle and ending sounds.
- A poem often has rhythm. This means it has a regular pattern of beats that you can hear.
- As you read "Under a Rock" and "Night Song," think about rhyme and rhythm.

Read Together

Under a Rock

Lift up a rock
and you will see
a busy bug
community.

by Betsy Franco
illustrated by Chris Lensch

Night Song

When the sun has set
And night has come,
The insect chorus
Starts to hum.

And nothing else
Is there to hear,
But the insect voices
Soft and clear.

The insects hum
In sweet delight,
Singing their praises
Of the night.

by Leland B. Jacobs
illustrated by Chris Lensch

Let's Think About...

What are the **rhyming words** in each poem? Does each poem have **rhythm?** How can you tell?

Let's Think About...

How many lines are there in "Under a Rock"? How many stanzas are there in "Night Song"?

Let's Think About...

Reading Across Texts How are the bees in *Honey Bees* and the insects in these poems alike?

Writing Across Texts Write a short poem about insects. Use rhyming words and rhythm. Read your poem aloud.

Objectives

• Read fluently and understand texts at your grade level. • Identify and put words into groups based on what they mean. • Listen closely to speakers and ask questions to help you better understand the topic. • Share information and ideas about the topic. Speak at the correct pace. • Give instructions, follow directions, and retell those instructions in your own words. • Identify and use antonyms.

Read Together

Let's Learn It!

READING STREET ONLINE
VOCABULARY ACTIVITIES
www.ReadingStreet.com

Get Ready For Grade 2

Listen carefully when someone is giving directions.

Listening and Speaking

Follow Directions It is important to listen carefully to directions so that we can follow them correctly. Good listeners remember all the steps and can say them back.

Practice It! Listen to your teacher give directions on how to do jumping jacks. Listen carefully and say the steps back. Then follow the directions.

Vocabulary

An **antonym** is a word that means the opposite of another word.

***Full* is an antonym of *empty*.**

Practice It! Read the words. Write and say antonyms for each one.

hot **sad** **up** **day**

Fluency

Accuracy and Rate Read the sentences. When you read, say the word you see. Blend the sounds to read the word. Put the word in the sentence. Ask yourself if it makes sense.

Practice It!

1. Britt's family will go on a picnic.

2. Did you see some cute kittens?

3. Steve has a hat with three buttons.

My School

map
chalkboard
Cat
Dog
Frog
chalk
teacher
books
computer
eraser
ruler
pencils
scissors

clock
bulletin board
1 2 3 4 5
school
MIDDLETON HEIGHTS ELEMENTARY
playground
flag
student
crayon
cafeteria
table
classroom
chair
lunchbox

Where People Live

pueblo

cottage

apartment building

mobile home

log cabin

house

town house

houseboat

high-rise

Where Animals Live

den

barn

log

tree hollow

burrow

anthill

nest

hive

cave

doghouse

ocean

lodge

Where People Work

restaurant

construction site

farm

bank

store

office

hospital

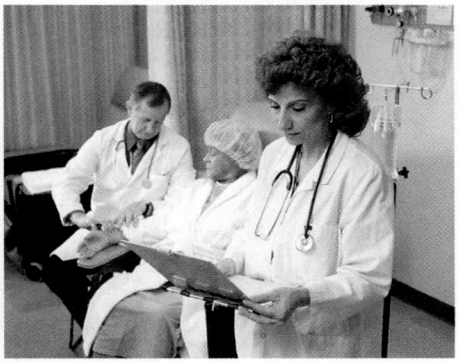

How People Play

music
basketball
33
football
dance
art

My Town
school
grocery store
School
bus driver
STOP
crossing guard
post office
mail carrier
garbage collector

barbershop
library
barber
librarian
cashier
bus stop
fire truck
firefighter
police officer
park
gardener

Max and Ruby: A Big Fish for Max

catch
good
no
put
said
want

Who Works Here?

live
out
people
who
work

The Farmer in the Hat

be
could
horse
of
old
paper

The Big Circle

down
inside
now
there
together

Honey Bees

also
family
new
other
some
their

Life in the Forest

around
find
food
grow
under
water

Acknowledgments

Text

Grateful acknowledgment is made to the following for copyrighted material:

Page 198: "Under a Rock" from *Thematic Poetry: Creepy Crawlies* by Betsy Franco. Scholastic Inc./Teaching Resources. Copyright © 2000 by Betsy Franco. Reprinted by permission.

Page 199: "Night Song" from *Just Around the Corner* by Leland B. Jacobs. © 1993 by Allan D. Jacobs. Reprinted by permission of Henry Holt and Company, LLC.

Note: Every effort has been made to locate the copyright owner of material reproduced on this component. Omissions brought to our attention will be corrected in subsequent editions.

Illustrations

Cover Daniel Moreton

14 Ethan Long

19 Kathi Ember

20-33 Jody Wheeler

46 O'Kif

52-64 Pat Cummings

80 Bill McGuire

90-99 Tim Spransy

101 April Mosakowski Hartmann

108 Susan Mitchell

112-126 Richard Bernal

132-135 Chris Boyd

144 Doug Holgate

164-167 Russell Farrell

178 Kellie Lewis

178-193 Tom Leonard

Photographs

Every effort has been made to secure permission and provide appropriate credit for photographic material. The publisher deeply regrets any omission and pledges to correct errors called to its attention in subsequent editions.

Unless otherwise acknowledged, all photographs are the property of Pearson Education, Inc.

Photo locators denoted as follows: Top (T), Center (C), Bottom (B), Left (L), Right (R), Background (Bkgd)

10 (B) ©Tom Stewart/Corbis

12 (B) Masterfile Corporation

16 Jupiter Images

42 Alistair Berg/Photonica/Getty Images

44 (B) ©LWA-Dann Tardif/Corbis

71 Wagner Farm, Glenview Park District, Glenview, IL.

72 (B) Wagner Farm, Glenview Park District, Glenview, IL.

74 (CR, CL) G K & Vikki Hart/Getty Images

75 (B) Melanie Acevedo/FoodPix/Jupiter Images

78 ©Jeremy Woodhouse/Getty Images

137 Digital Vision, Mark Downey/Getty Images, Tom Bean/Corbis

138 ©John Cornell/Getty Images

146 (Bkgd) Bill Ross/Corbis

147 (CL) ©Royalty-Free/Corbis, (TR) Photowood Inc./Corbis, (TL) Steve Kaufman/Corbis

148 (BL) Tom Uhlman/Visuals Unlimited

151 (TR) Fritz Polking/Visuals Unlimited

152 (T) Jamie Harron; Papilio/Corbis

154 (T) Stephen Dalton/Photo Researchers, Inc.

155 (TR) Gerard Fuehrer/Visuals Unlimited, (B) Getty Images

156 (T) Jim Clare/Nature Picture Library

157 (T) Frederick D. Atwood

158 (CL) ©Gary W. Carter/Corbis, (BR) ©Royalty-Free/Corbis, (TL) Bill Dyer/Photo Researchers, Inc., (TR) Melissa Farlow/Aurora & Quanta Productions

159 (TL) Stephen Krasemann/Getty Images, (BR) Tim Thompson/Corbis

167 (C) Theo Allofs/Danita Delimont, Agent

168 Vernon Leach/Alamy

170 ©Premaphotos/Nature Picture Library

201 (TL) ©Jonelle Weave/Getty Images, (TR) Jupiter Image.

High-Frequency Words

Identify and read the high-frequency words that you have learned this year. How many words can you read?

Unit R.1
a
green
I
see

Unit R.2
like
one
we

Unit R.3
do
look
was
yellow
you

Unit R.4
are
have
that
they
two

Unit R.5
he
is
three
to
with

Unit R.6
for
go
here
me
where

Unit 1.1
come
my
way

Unit 1.2
she
take
up
what

Unit 1.3
blue
from
help
little
use

Unit 1.4
eat
five
four
her
this
too

Unit 1.5
saw
small
tree
your

Unit 1.6
home
into
many
them

Unit 2.1
catch
good
no
put
said
want

Unit 2.2
be
could
horse
of
old
paper

Unit 2.3
live
out
people
who
work

Unit 2.4
down
inside
now
there
together

Unit 2.5
around
find
food
grow
under
water

Unit 2.6
also
family
new
other
some
their

Unit 3.1
always
become
day
everything
nothing
stays
things

Unit 3.2
any
enough
ever
every
own
sure
were

Unit 3.3
away
car
friends
house
our
school
very

Unit 3.4
afraid
again
few
how
read
soon

Unit 3.5
done
know
push
visit
wait

Unit 3.6
before
does
good-bye
oh
right
won't

Unit 4.1
about
enjoy
gives
surprise
worry
would

Unit 4.2
colors
draw
drew
great
over
show
sign

Unit 4.3
found
mouth
once
took
wild

Unit 4.4
above
eight
laugh
moon
touch

Unit 4.5
picture
remember
room
stood
thought

Unit 4.6
across
because
dance
only
opened
shoes
told

Unit 5.1
along
behind
eyes
never
pulling
toward

Unit 5.2
door
loved
should
wood

Unit 5.3
among
another
instead
none

Unit 5.4
against
goes
heavy
kinds
today

Unit 5.5
built
early
learn
science
through

Unit 5.6
answered
carry
different
poor